D1234605

Simon Says

Simon Says

TAILS TOLD BY
THE RED LION INN AMBASSADOR

By Jana Laiz & Jayne Church
Photography by Nancy-Fay Hecker

Crow Flies Press • South Egremont, MA

CROW FLIES PRESS
PO BOX 614   SOUTH EGREMONT, MA 01258   (413)-281-7015
www.crowfliespress.com
publisher@crowfliespress.com

Simon Says: Tails Told by The Red Lion Inn Ambassador
ISBN 978-0-9814910-3-5
Copyright © 2015 Crow Flies Press
Simon logo by Ken Musselman ~ kenmusselman.com
Cover and page design by Anna Myers ~ anna-myers.com
Printed in the USA

Dedication

To the memory of my precious Siamese cat,
Tamina who will be forever in my heart.
~Jana Laiz

For the most recent bunch: Patches, Ollie, Aruba,
Raylen and for all the ones who have gone before.
Most especially for the two loves of my life,
GCIII and Jen. I love you bunches.
~Jayne Church

For my parents with deep love and gratitude—
Mimi with a courageous, generous heart full of wonder
and Angus who loved a grand hotel and was by
my side when I first met Simon.
~Nancy-Fay Hecker

Simon Says

TAILS TOLD BY THE RED LION INN AMBASSADOR

Catpurr One

An Introduction

*M*y name is Simon. Simon Treadway Gato. I came to The Red Lion Inn quite a number of years ago and found the place so entirely to my liking that I never left. The staff treats me like royalty and I am well known among guests and workers alike. I am greeted daily by name. "Hello Simon!" "How are you, Simon?" "Nice to see you, Simon!" "Ambassador Simon! So good to see you!" I return each greeting with a simple nod of acknowledgment.

Ambassador. I do enjoy that title. It is an honor to be called that since The Red Lion Inn is one

of the oldest and most respected inns in what we locals like to call "The Shire," or as tourists and outsiders call "The Berkshires." It is located in the town of Stockbridge made famous by the Mahican Indians who lived here long ago, by Norman Rockwell who painted scenes of this charming New England town, and by that popular James Taylor song ~ *Sweet Baby James*.

Built circa 1773, it is a grand hotel, elegant, with an air of comfortable formality but completely without pretense. There are one hundred twenty-five bedrooms and an enormous number of fireplaces, a tavern, a cozy living room filled with comfy chairs, chaise longues, a shabby sofa or two, a very posh dining room where the most delicious dishes are served, a huge kitchen, where those dishes are prepared…

And a wonderfully warm basement ~ that is where I live.

You might wonder how this fancy inn's oldest permanent resident and ambassador could live in the basement. Well, I love it down there. It offers privacy when I need it, lovely spaces in which to sprawl out and relax, hiding places for when I am feeling my most antisocial, and the presence of the occasional mouse. Don't be alarmed. Even the finest hotels are not without the infrequent itinerant rodent. And by the way, have I mentioned that I'm a cat?

photo by Jayne Church

No? Well, I am the only cat on the premises, and although I spent some time in a shelter with other felines, having been put there by my former allergic owners, I hardly know what to say about it. I am surrounded by humans. I will say, however, that if ever there was a lucky cat, I think it might be me. And that is all due to the woman I will refer to as "Mom" for the remainder of this journal.

Mom works here at the Inn. Her job is to manage the shop, her office is my home: the basement. She likes it down there now as much as I do, but before I came she had been feeling lonely, with no cat to snuggle or curl up with, or to catch that occasional mouse that caused her to jump up on one of the many boxes stacked down there. So one day, she went to a local animal shelter ~ The Eleanor

Sonsini Shelter in Pittsfield, a town some miles from here. I imagine Eleanor was as kind a woman as Mom is. Mom went to the shelter to look for a cat that would be just right for such a place as this. She deliberated for hours, talking to every feline she laid eyes on, and although I knew I was the right cat for the job all along and wondered what was taking her so long, I was patient and hopeful and perfectly ready when she finally made her decision and chose me. I bade my fare-thee-wells and allowed myself to be placed into the carrier that would bring me to my new life, whatever that might be. And I could not have dreamed what awaited me!

Can you imagine what it was like for me? From cage to castle in the blink of an eye. Some might call it luck, others serendipity. But as soon as I arrived, I knew it was my destiny. I do admit, there was a period of adjustment. I mean, I was behind bars for a number of months, and although the shelter had playrooms and lots of handlers to pet and fuss over me, I went from rags to riches overnight. There simply had to be some time to take it all in.

And so at first, I hid, spending most of my time below stairs, where my little apartment is, finding all manner of cubbies and hidey-holes and corners where I could curl up in relative safety and purr myself to sleep. Mom was always there, constant as the morning sun, smiling at me, feeding me tidbits of delicious food, encouraging me to hop up on her lap when I finally allowed myself that luxury. After getting to know and trust Mom and having nearly exhausted my exploration of the basement, she gently coaxed me to venture up the stairs to explore the rest of the house, one room at a time.

The first time I tentatively entered the lobby, the sheer number of people overwhelmed me. Shoes and boots and heels and sneakers running here and there (remember, I have a cat's eye view) and I had

to avoid being trampled on several occasions. And so many hands reaching for me! Of course, I understood my appeal, I mean, who wouldn't want to pet me? These days, I make every effort to be courteous when I am being held, handled and loved, but those first days, well, they were scary and I often wiggled away to escape, heading right back to my subterranean safe haven. On one particularly affectionate afternoon, I needed to get away from all the admirers and tried to get downstairs, but the door was firmly closed and Mom was nowhere in sight. I became rather frantic and headed up the stairs, which was then off-limits, and I admit, I may have broken some piece or other of bric-a-brac.

Well, the very next day Mom arranged for the maintenance crew, bless their souls, to install a tiny door, just big enough for me and me alone leading to my apartments. Mom taught me how to use it, and now it is my getaway, and I am not ashamed, Ambassador notwithstanding.

Catpurr Two

The Rules I Have to Follow at The Red Lion Inn

*T*here are many rules at this fine hotel, rules for the guests and for the staff, but these particular rules apply to me, although if a *human* were to break any of these, they might be removed from the property.

* Never eat the flowers on the tables, even if they taste scrumptious. Mom says they can make me sick and throw up. Cats do throw up; it's what we do best, after sleeping. Throwing up at The Red Lion Inn is frowned upon.

* Never flex my claws on the furniture. Yes, I do have my own huge and deliciously scratchable scratching post in the Side Parlor. But whenever there's some special event  in there, it gets moved somewhere else. It's just way too much trouble to go looking for it when the nice, soft, armchairs are right there. Oh well. Scratching The Red Lion Inn's sofas is frowned upon.

*   Never ever ever set foot in the dining room. Ever. Especially during the dinner hour. Really. Not even once. (If you think you see me in there, it is a figment of your imagination.)

*   Never sit outside a guest's room at midnight and cry to be let in. Forbidden.

* Never set foot in a guest room. Ever. Or hide under the bed and refuse to leave. (And never, ever tell if a guest lets you in...)

* Never hunt down a bird on the front walk at noon on a bright summer's day in full view of dozens of guests rocking in chairs on the porch. It might prove unsettling.

Catpurr Three

A Few More Things to Know About Me

I Simon, The Red Lion Inn cat, am a great many things. I am smart, funny, cuddly and bi-lingual. While I still speak cat fluently as my native tongue, I understand English as well as the next fellow. If I do not respond to you, it is because I am choosing not to.

* I weigh 15 pounds on a good day. Every day is a good day.

* I came to The Red Lion Inn in 2006 when I was 3 years old. You do the math.

* I was adopted from a local "no kill" shelter. I approve of "no kill" shelters.

* I can often be found on the 4th floor. It's lovely up there.

* I don't like to be picked up. I mean it.

* I love to be scratched under my chin. Honestly. Love.

* I don't like people food. Not tempted. Nope. Not at all. Never.

* I eat both wet and dry cat food. Yum.

* I have my own Facebook page. Please "like" me.

* I love kitty treats and cat-nip. No, they do not make me crazy. Yes they do. No they don't. Yes…

* Mom says I might have food allergies, so if you want to bring me a treat, which I hope you will, please get the stamp of approval from Mom, would you?

* My favorite toy is the laser light. There. No, there… Mom will lend you her

laser if you want to play with me! There it is…oh, no there….

* I love greeting guests and will pose for pictures if asked nicely. Nicely.

* I think tummy rubs are lovely. Don't you?

* I am not allowed in the guest rooms, no matter what I tell you. Did I say that? Don't listen to me. (Mom says listen to me!)

* In the winter I spend most of my time sleeping on radiators. They are warm.

* I love to sleep…zzz. Sometimes all day and I don't like to be disturbed when I am in dreamland. Zzzzz….

* I will find the tiniest spot of sunshine to bask in. Pardon me, if you could not stand on that spot…

* I like nice, calm children. Calm. Nice. Well-behaved. I really do.

* If I'm by the door, please let me in or out. Don't worry. I'll be just fine. I want to keep my nine lives intact.

* When the Inn is very crowded I disappear. You will never find me.

Catpurr Four

Anecdotes About Me by Mom

One morning Simon and I were communing near the Side Parlor in The Red Lion Inn. Facing each other, from the corner of my eye, I noticed a woman sitting in a chair, just in the Side Parlor doorway. She was trying, with no luck, to get a photo of Simon, without getting up from her chair. Simon paid no attention to her at all. After a little while of watching her struggle, I turned to Simon and said, "Simon, this nice lady is trying to take your picture. Why don't you be a good cat and be more cooperative." I could see him considering what I said (as I mentioned, we commune)

and then he stood up. He turned and walked over to the lady in question, sat down directly in front of her and paused while she snapped the picture. Then, without moving his body, he turned his head to the left, held it and then turned to the right and held that pose. The woman was able to get a front shot and two perfect profiles. Simon then stood up, turned and walked away. He winked at me; telling me that it was another job well done and he could take a break.

*

Here's a "dirty" little story...a litter box tale. I'm a bit embarrassed to mention it, but it does Simon such credit that I will swallow my dignity and report it. I try, as do all good cat owners, to clean out the litter box daily. It was a particularly busy day and I decided to leave the litter until later. I went upstairs to work and when I came back down to the basement, I noticed that the litter box had moved, nearly a foot from its place. I assumed someone had knocked it by accident, though not many people ever come down here. I moved it back and continued my work. When I passed it next, a few hours later, it had moved several feet from its original spot. And there was Simon, tail swishing in disgruntlement. I cleaned the box! And continue to do so, and this has never happened again. Smart guy. ~ *Mom*.

Catpurr Five

About Mom by Me

About Mom. I'm not saying Mom is neurotic. I would never say that, and certainly, no one knows better than Mom that cats should never be allowed out. But during my first year at the Inn she did everything she could to keep me inside. I mean everything. She posted signs on all the doors in the employee areas~ DO NOT LET THE CAT OUT! She reminded everyone she saw not to let me out~ DO NOT LET THE CAT OUT! Most of all she worried and worried and watched the doors and worried some more. SHUT THE DOOR! I'M WORRIED HE'LL GET OUT!

But then, one bright summery day, while she was watching and worrying and worrying and watching, Mom realized that she could never watch all of the doors all of the time. I CAN NEVER WATCH EVERY DOOR IN THE INN. IT'S IMPOSSIBLE! WHAT DO I DO?

While she was keeping her eagle eye on the front door, someone was coming in the side door and someone else was going out the porch door. She looked like I do when I watch that pesky red light that appears and disappears. Watching Mom's distress, I knew I had to do something to calm her down. I waited until a door opened right near Mom and I walked to it, looked out, but stayed in. I walked away, surreptitiously brushing Mom's leg as I passed by. For her sake. For sanity's sake.

And Mom relaxed. She calmed down and began to trust me because she understood that I'm a very smart cat. Mom says I'm the smartest cat she's ever known. And she should know, she's always had a houseful of cats in her own home-away-from-here.

So yes, I am smart, smart enough to stay close to the Inn and out of the road. There are loud, fast, huge, smelly cars racing by out there on that road. Nope, that road is not safe for cats, no matter how smart we are. ~ *Simon*

A Few More Things to Know About Me, by Me

I have had to be rescued a few times, by a kindly maintenance man or housekeeper, when I could not escape from a particularly creative hiding place, but mostly my scaredy-catness has been replaced by a cat curiosity that will not be denied. And once I overcame my fear and natural cat-dislike of change, I learned to enjoy making new friends and discovering new hidey-holes and sleeping spots in unexpected places.

Under the Lincoln portrait in the Side Parlor is wonderful. What a good man he was and I

enjoy sleeping under that fine photograph. There is a comfy red fainting couch on the fourth floor that is a particular favorite. I'm embarrassed to share this, but you can see the indent of my body on that chaise. Delicious. And of course, the porch's white wicker. Ever a favorite.

You might say that I found my calling as Lobby Ambassador here at The Red Lion Inn. I love to greet people and make them feel welcome. I love

to pose for photos. I love to mingle with the guests and allow them to rub my tummy. On very, very rare occasions I may even jump into a friendly lap and purr.

I take my job seriously. While many cats would find the responsibility burdensome, perhaps even objectionable, I enjoy it and take great pride in a job well done. Crowds of people milling about and over-excited children chasing me can be overwhelming, so summers and holidays are particularly stressful times. Still, I stick with it as long as I can before retreating to my apartments below. More often than not, Mom is there, ready to stroke me, and talk softly to me, which always settles me down. Then I get into my comfortable duck-pose (tummy on floor, paws tucked under chest and bottom, tail wrapped around) on the floor next to her and let her calming presence soothe me until it's time to go up and face the crowds again.

I'm very good at sniffing out the "cat-person" in the crowd and they become my Human-For-The-Day. I like to sit with them by the fire and let them scratch me under my chin. I escort them to

their room and help them settle in. Many of my Humans come back year after year to visit me and have become lasting friends. (A big hello-meow to

Amy, Mike, Simone, Charles, Patressa, Judi, Mike and Lynn. Forgive me if I left anyone out…you know who you are. Meowah!!)

Catpurr Seven

The Outdoors

When I do go out in the warm weather, namely spring, summer and fall, (I don't do winter, thank you) I like to curl up in one of the wicker chairs in the side Piazza and doze in the sun. Sometimes I walk around our block, visiting neighbors, popping into the local shops to check on business, or I stop into the bank for a quick cool off. I'm always greeted with smiles and gentle pats everywhere I go, from old friends and strangers alike. I often nap in the shade of the flowerbeds on the walk in front of the Inn. It's so pleasant to drift off among the flowers, to hear the murmur of

voices and passing footsteps strolling by. I can hear little birds and chipmunks twitter and chatter, a peaceful sound at a distance. I remember the rules and try my hardest to keep my eyes closed and not pounce. We wouldn't want to upset any guests watching from the rocking chairs on the porch.

Our street is lined with trees. There is a library at the corner with lovely shops in between. People are always there, each and every season, taking photos of our historic town center. I have never ventured further than 'round the block, but I imagine all sorts of lovely places to hide and trees to climb. But my work is at the Inn, so I stay within its boundaries.

During the cold months things are quiet here. There are fewer guests and I can nap to my heart's content in the patch of morning sunshine near the back door, or in the afternoon on the first floor landing. When it's quiet and cold I also love to settle in for a long nap on the couch in front of the fireplace or on the radiator across from the Gift Shop.

One winter, though, I did cause a bit of drama. Mom was gone for a short vacation and though I rarely go out in the cold, I was bored. Without Mom here to rub my tummy or play the red-light game with me, I decided to venture out into the nippy day to see what I could see. I had made the rounds of the parking lot and was heading back to warm my paws when quite out of nowhere a strange cat popped out of the shadows right in front of me. I'm considered large for a cat but this one was a BIG Tom, smoky gray with scary black stripes. He had a bend in his tail, a chunk out of his ear, and a very unpleasant look on his face. He didn't greet me politely

as I would expect, instead he arched his back, curled his lip and extended his claws in a rather menacing way. "GrrrrrrrrrRRRRRRRRRRRRRRRRRRRoooooooow-wwwwwrrrrrrrrLLL*!@!*^" he pronounced, rudely.

Taken aback, what could I do but answer in kind! I arched my back, puffed out my tail, stood up on my front paws and replied, "RRRRRRRRRRrrrr-rrrrrHIssssSSSSSSSggrerrrrrowwwwwwwXXX!!" letting him know just who was in charge. Well, that devil cat leapt at me, growling and clawing. I jumped at him and my superior strength and fighting skills soon sent him running, but not before he had taken a nip from my left flank.

I ran down to my bed and stayed there, licking my wounds, waiting for Mom to return, feeling somewhat triumphant but also a little sorry for myself. It hurt.

By the time Mom returned several days later, the nip was raw, red and clearly infected. She took me to my doctor, a kind man who smelled pleasantly like sawdust. He gave me a shot (a long needle…but I am brave) and instructed Mom to rub ointment on me and feed me pills every day. He told Mom that I was very lucky, and that she was good for keeping my shots up to date. Had she not taken such excellent care of me, I would have had to be quarantined for 45 days since they had no

idea who had bitten me. And though I wished I could tell them whodunnit, I didn't see that Tom again, so I kept quiet.

Catpurr Eight

Ta Ta For Now
(cats like to say that)

Over my many years of living at this magnificent and historic inn, as I patrol the grounds and wander my neighborhood, I've made friends with a few of my own kind. That BIG Tom never did return, I'm happy to say, but it is nice to see a friendly furry face on occasion. We are proud Stockbridge cats. My pals often look at me with awe, yet I notice a look of pity in their eyes as they look at me. They wonder and have asked me if I would not have been happier spending my life with a human family, as they do,

sharing one of those small but cozy houses with a real mom, a dad and one or two children to play with. And I honestly say that my answer would have to be a decided "no!" I may not have a dad or kiddies but I do have a mom who loves me very much.

While I don't have a cozy cottage to call home, look at what I do have: hundreds of beautiful rooms filled with soft chairs and downy beds, sofas, pillows, fireplaces, rugs and curtains to sleep on, climb on, hide under, curl up in front of and stretch out on. I have countless places to hide in and an apartment to call my own.

I ask them, how many cats do you know who actually have a job, other than chasing mice? They look at me strangely, but do not reply. I tell them, not only do I have a job I adore, I have a position of respect and responsibility. I am the Lobby Ambassador of The Red Lion Inn. I greet hundreds of guests, I escort them to their rooms and I make sure that they're comfortable. I let them stroke and pet me all day long, even when I may be a bit out of sorts. I pose for pictures. And, while I don't have a family in the true sense, I have more humans who love me than I can count. Yes, I am loved by many, and I love them all in return. I don't tell them this, as I am as humble as a cat can be, but I am happier than any cat ever was and I expect to be here in this wonderful forever home... well, forever.

'Til next time…

Acknowledgments

Enormous thanks to Ken Musselman for his charming Simon logo and for the many colorful portraits of The Red Lion Inn, which mostly include Simon front and center.

To Carol Lew for her amazing portrait of Simon all dressed up for his role as Lobby Ambassador. We think Carol caught the essence of Simon and his unique cattitude in her painting.

And most especially to The Red Lion Inn (www.redlioninn.com), its staff and C.E.O. Sarah Eustis for providing Simon with his beautiful, safe and loving home. He is, indeed, the luckiest cat in the world.

Thanks to Anna Myers for cheerfully pulling our ideas together from different directions and creating something wonderful. Sincere appreciation goes to Crow Flies Press for making this book a reality.

And to Simon. You are such a charmingly cool cat and make so many people happy. We are eternally grateful to you for allowing us to tell your story in words and pictures.

Thanks to our family and friends who love and encourage us every day in so many ways.

~ The Authors & The Photographer

About the Authors

Jana Laiz is an award-winning author and the mom of two cats, two dogs, and two kids. She got her first cat, Irving, when she was five and has had a plethora of animals ever since.
www.janalaiz.com

Jayne Church When Jayne isn't busy managing the Gift Shop at The Red Lion Inn she's at home with her ever encouraging and loving husband, George Church III, four curious cats and a blind dachshund named Missy.

Nancy-Fay Hecker shares a love for life through photography. Her family, including pups and kitties present and past, all inspire her creative spirit. Her company, Apple Hill Designs, publishes scenic cards and mementos.
www.applehilldesigns.com

Simon Treadway Gato

Born in The Berkshires in April 2003, Simon came to his forever home at The Red Lion Inn in 2006 where he holds the esteemed position of Lobby Ambassador, greeting guests and spreading joy wherever he goes.